HARRY BELAFONTE

A Little Golden Book® Biography

By Lavaille Lavette
Illustrated by Anastasia Magloire Williams

 A GOLDEN BOOK • NEW YORK

Copyright © 2023 by Lavette Books, Inc.
All rights reserved. Published in the United States by Golden Books, an imprint of Random House Children's Books, a division of Penguin Random House LLC, 1745 Broadway, New York, NY 10019, by arrangement with EBONY JR!, an imprint of Ebony Media Publishing, LLC, and Lavette Books, Inc. Golden Books, A Golden Book, A Little Golden Book, the G colophon, and the distinctive gold spine are registered trademarks of Penguin Random House LLC. EBONY JR! and the EBONY JR! colophon are registered trademarks of Ebony Media.
rhcbooks.com
ebonymagazinepublishing.com
lavettebooks.com
Educators and librarians, for a variety of teaching tools, visit us at RHTeachersLibrarians.com
Library of Congress Control Number: 2022931682
ISBN 978-0-593-56810-1 (trade) — ISBN 978-0-593-56811-8 (ebook)
Printed in the United States of America
10 9 8 7 6 5 4 3 2 1
First Edition

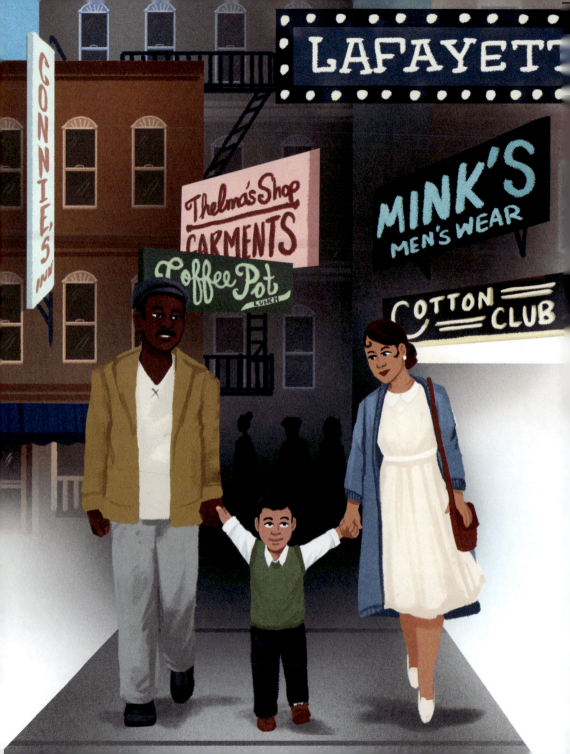

Harry Belafonte

is a beloved entertainer and civil rights hero who fought for equal rights for African Americans.

Harold George Belafonte was born on March 1, 1927, in Harlem, New York. His parents called him Harry. Harry's mother, Melvine, and father, Harold, were both from island nations in the Caribbean. But when Harry was a little boy, they lived in the big, busy city. His mother worked as a house cleaner, and his father worked as a cook on a ship.

When Harry was about nine years old, he left Harlem to live with his grandmother in Jamaica. There, Harry discovered an upbeat, joyful kind of music called calypso.

Life in Jamaica was different from the fast-paced life of Harlem. At night, Harry would often climb a mango tree. While snacking on the fruit, he would listen to the calypso music ringing through the streets below as he stared up at the bright stars.

When Harry was a teenager, he moved from Jamaica back to New York to live with his mother.

Life in New York seemed unfair. African American people were not treated as equal citizens. They were not allowed to stay at the same hotels, eat at the same restaurants, or even attend the same schools as white people.

Harry's mother believed that everyone should be treated the same. She taught him to stand up for what's right and to fight for fair treatment.

Harry was a member of the track team at his high school. In 1944, he left school before graduating to join the United States Navy.

He hoped that the horrors of World War II would change people—that they would be kinder to those who were different from them. But that was not the case.

When the war ended, Harry returned home and got a job working as a janitor in an apartment building.

One day, a tenant gave Harry tickets to the American Negro Theatre. It was a gift that changed his life. Inspired by what he saw, Harry vowed to become a performer.

Harry took acting lessons in the Dramatic Workshop at the New School. In order to pay for classes, Harry performed as a singer at night clubs around the city.

In December 1953, when he was twenty-six years old, Harry performed in his first Broadway musical—*John Murray Anderson's Almanac*. The next year, he won a Tony Award for his role.

A Tony is an award given for excellence in theater.

Harry loved acting, but music launched his career. People in the record business noticed Harry's joyful performances at the Royal Roost jazz club. They offered him a record deal, and in 1956, Harry released an album called *Calypso*. That album captured his love for the music he enjoyed as a boy in Jamaica.

Calypso was so loved that it became the first album ever to sell over one million copies. That success allowed him to release more albums, and in 1961, he won a Grammy Award for his album *Swing Dat Hammer*. Then in 1966, Harry won another Grammy for his album *An Evening with Belafonte/Makeba*.

A Grammy is an award given for excellence in music.

Harry's success went well beyond music and the theater. In 1960, he won an Emmy Award for his performance in the television special *Tonight with Belafonte*, when he was a guest host for *The Tonight Show*.

Harry became the first African American to win an Emmy. His career was soaring, but he wanted to do more to help people. Harry decided to use his fame to inspire others to change the world.

An Emmy is an award given for excellence in television.

Harry met civil rights leader Dr. Martin Luther King Jr. at a church in Harlem. The two became close friends.

Harry worked with Dr. King to inspire others to stand up for their rights in a peaceful way. He donated money to the Civil Rights Movement and helped raise money for the cause. He also helped Dr. King organize the 1963 March on Washington, where a quarter-million people saw Dr. King give his famous "I Have a Dream" speech. This event put pressure on lawmakers to make laws more fair.

Harry's activism made him a leader in the Civil Rights Movement. This was not always good for his career as a performer. Many people did not like that he was speaking out, and some people in Hollywood did not want to work with him. But Harry knew that his words—and his civil rights work—were important.

"Peace is necessary."
—Harry Belafonte

In the 1980s, there was a shortage of food in parts of Africa. When Harry learned that millions of people were going hungry, he knew he had to do something. He helped organize a group of famous musicians to sing a song called "We Are the World." The song was released in 1985, and it raised money for people in need in Africa.

Harry also bravely spoke out about issues that Black people faced in South Africa. A policy called apartheid forced Black people to live and work separately from white people and in poor conditions.

Harry organized a concert in London to raise money and bring the world's attention to the problem. He worked with South African leaders, such as Nelson Mandela, to end apartheid.

Harry received a special Oscar at the 2014 Academy Awards called the Jean Hersholt Humanitarian Award. This honor is given to movie artists who make important contributions to help people live safer, healthier lives.

In 2017, there was a celebration in Harlem, Harry's childhood neighborhood, to honor his accomplished life. At ninety years old, Harry stood beside the mayor of New York City, other elected officials, and friends as they unveiled a plaque with the local library's new name—Harry Belafonte 115th Street Library.

Harry Belafonte is an inspiration to people all over the world. He has shown us that we can do what we love while taking actions to make the world a kinder, fairer place.

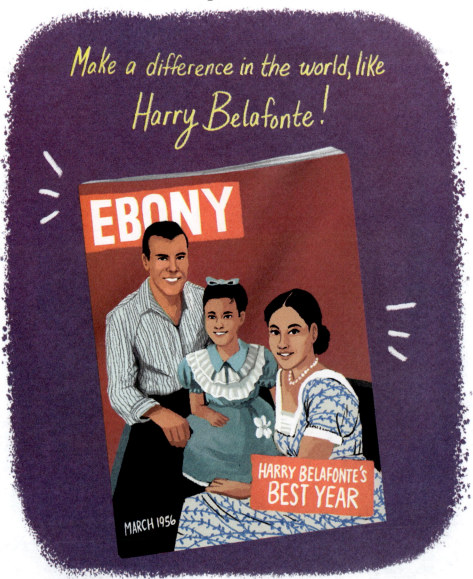